Ghastlies,
Goops & Pincushions

Some Other Books by X. J. Kennedy

The Forgetful Wishing Well: Poems for Young People
The Owlstone Crown
Brats
(Margaret K. McElderry Books)

Knock at a Star: A Child's Introduction to Poetry
(with Dorothy M. Kennedy)
Did Adam Name the Vinegarroon?

Ghastlies, Goops & Pincushions
NONSENSE VERSE

X. J. Kennedy
drawings by Ron Barrett

Margaret K. McElderry Books
New York

Thanks

Cricket, the magazine for children, first printed "A Giraffe's Laughs Last."

Barbara Dubivsky, who edited a feature of limericks in the *New York Times Magazine* to mark Edward Lear's birthday in 1987, first printed "A luckless time-traveler from Lynn."

Norma Farber and Myra Cohn Livingston, editors of *These Small Stones* (A Charlotte Zolotow Book/Harper & Row), first accepted "Things on a Microscope Slide."

Timbuktu first printed "Agatha Ghastly Makes Light of Auntie," "Special Flavor," "Supper Stratagem," "Trimmed-down Tales," and "What We Might Be, What We Are."

Robert Wallace, editor of *Sometime the Cow Kick Your Head: Light Year '88–9* (Bits Press), first printed "Long-distance Call" and "Weems Ghastly's Goodies."

"Italian Noodles" expands on a short poem, "Lasagna," previously printed in *The Phantom Ice Cream Man* (A Margaret K. McElderry Book/Atheneum, 1979).

Dorothy Kennedy supplied a closing rhyme.

Gelett Burgess, American writer and illustrator (1866–1951), invented the word *goop.*

Contents

Guinevere, where's brother Peter?
Tied fast to the parking meter.
Don't worry, Mom, I stuck a dime
Down him. He's still got lots of time.

Basketball Bragging

Agatha Goop with a whale of a whoop
Swept a swisher through the hoop.

She told her teammates, "There you are!
You guys are dog meat! I'm the star!"

Her teammates knew just what to do:
They dribbled her down and dunked her through.

Now Agatha's nose may be out of joint,
But she had to admit that they'd made their point.

The Vacuum Cleaner's Swallowed Will

The vacuum cleaner's swallowed Will.
  He's vanished. What a drag!
Still, we can do without him till
  It's time to change the bag.

Sheepshape

I shear sheep in all sorts of shapes
Like shooting stars and spangles.
I shear them in the shapes of apes.
My ewe has four right angles.

I give some sheep a camel's back,
Two mountains and a valley.
I make short shrift of them with shears.
Me, I don't shilly-shally.

I shear sheep short. Their wiry wool
Is well worthwhile to save.
Oh, what sheer joy it is to give
A shaggy sheep a shave!

Babbling baby, left alone,
Punched some buttons on the phone.

Poppa paid for her to coo
All the way to Katmandu.

Word of Warning

Never put mustard on your auk
Or it might clam up and not talk
Or, what's worse, when you're soundly snoring,
Shake you awake to say, "You're boring."

No! Don't put mustard on your auk!
For if you do you'll hear it squawk,
"I've got to run down to the cleaners.
What do you think we auks are? Wieners?"

Robert Robot, go unscrew
Your burnt-out head, stick in a new!

Floss your filthy teeth with wire!
Go oil your nose! Shoeshine your tire!

Don't stand there like a screwloose dolt!
Pick up a wrench and twist your bolt!

Light your lightbulb! Look alive!
Dust your dirty old disk drive!

Aunt Gilda's Pincushion Head

Aunt Gilda wears twelve hat pins
All sticking out, so that
Those pesky crows with scratchy toes
Won't lay eggs in her hat.

The gnomes of Nome
Are not at home
    To prying human eyes.
They live in a dome
Of frozen foam
    On cold icicle pies.

The gnomes of Nome
Dislike to roam.
    To them, a blizzard's pleasing,
And when a gnome
Feels most at home
    He howls, "Hot dog! I'm freezing!"

Special Flavor

While filling cones, Disgustus Goop
Leaned down so deep to take a scoop,
He fell headfirst with dreadful shriek
Into the flavor of the week.

The manager, a man of taste,
Said, "This ice cream's too good to waste.
The cops had better not come bust us
For selling butternut Disgustus."

Never stand under an anvil,
Never accept a strange box,
And never step under a landslide—
That rain on your head might be rocks.

Expect to meet man-eating lions
Whose escape is announced on the news.
Don't ever hold on to a round thing
With a fast-burning, sputtering fuse.

Don't argue with little green Martians,
Don't shake and roll dynamite dice.
Train your tomcat in telling the difference
Between kangaroos and house mice.

Watch out for Tasmanian devils,
Stay indoors when your nights have full moons,
And you might have a chance at surviving
In the world of old movie cartoons!

A Giraffe's Laughs Last

When spied on in a zoo, Giraffe
   Neglects his tree-leaf diet
To take a look at you and laugh—
   Your short neck! What a riot!

He grins and grins from ear to ear.
   If you've not yet departed,
In several days you'll get to hear
   The throaty laugh you started.

One day Snow Leopard caught a cough
And sneezed so hard his spots fell off.

Now every time it starts in snowing,
Don't look for him. He won't be showing.

Whistler's Father

Whistler's mother—she's world famous
From a painting by her son.
What became of Whistler's father?
He's the seldom mentioned one.

What does Whistler's father look like
Propped up in his straight-backed chair?
Does he whisper through white whiskers?
Has he wisps of whisk-broom hair?

Whistler's father, stiffly collared,
In the fussiest of coats
With his penknife, sitting whittling
Fleets of little wooden boats,

Whistling softly with his whistler
Long, low whistles—can that be
Whistler's father? If I ask him,
Will he whittle one for me?

Skunk cabbage slaw has one bad flaw—
It's tough to gnaw a jawful.
You chaw and chaw. It's rough when raw,
But cooked, it smells just awful.

Skunk cabbage slaw! Don't make it, Maw!
For weeks we've chomped and chomped,
But all these green and swamp-grown leaves
Leave (groan!) our stomachs swamped.

I like to shuffle in my socks
   Across our scuffy carpet
And touch Aunt Sue and give her shocks.
   I gave her one so sharp it

Caused her to shoot out of her shoes
   With—wow!—a big blue spark.
Now Auntie Sue's the bulb we use
   To read by after dark.

My Uncle Demented, he's invented
More stuff than Thomas Edison—
Like frozen spinach on a stick,
Like hot marshmallow medicine.

He's built a kettle for your stove
That burps instead of whistles.
It fixes flats in popped balloons
And brushes toothbrush bristles.

He's made a pair of wooden shoes
For a one-legged stork,
A gadget to remove King Kongs
From rooftops in New York,

A paper airplane nine miles long,
And even paper diapers
That can't be ripped and come equipped
With built-in windshield wiapers.

A Misspent Youth

The Ugly Duckling's shoulders sag.
"I've tried, but paddling's such a drag.
I just can't get a web to grow
Between my great and second toe.
My head won't throw back when I drink.
I try to swim, I just plain sink.
Oh, I'm the crummiest of quackers.
Though I get by on soda crackers,
To scoop a bug up out of ooze
Just makes me want to sing the blues.
I can't wait till I grow up big."

What duckling? He's a suckling pig.

With his hand-cranked freezer Weems
Makes the ghastliest ice creams:
Chocolate toothpaste, cherry chunk
(Chock full of pits), vanilla skunk,
Parsnip garbage, radish trash,
Butter toucan, hellish hash—
He who samples Weems's cones
Crumples to a heap and groans;
Anyone who's ever poked
Spoon in bullfrog sherbert's croaked.

The Horn on Our Pickup Truck Stayed Stuck

The horn on our pickup truck
Stayed stuck—
    All night it went on beeping.
The neighbors all
Began to bawl,
    "Hey, knock it off! We're sleeping!"

The firemen sprayed
Some foam and made
    Our poor truck cease to bellow,
But now we ride
To school inside
    A gooey white marshmallow.

1

A big red apple! Who'd refuse?
So Snow White bites and takes a snooze.
Her Dwarfs shed tears for seven years.
The Prince goes *smack!*—her windpipe clears.

2

Rapunzel, let me down your hair,
　The one way to be trusted
To hoist me up from here to there—
　The elevator's busted.

Trouble with Baby

Now why did Mother go and teach
Her little tot karate?
With one shot of his foot he's smashed
To smithereens his potty.

With piercing screams he's gone and chopped
In two his high-chair tray
And in a temper tantrum flung
The TV set away.

The longest lizard,
Diplodocus,
Had hammer teeth with which to knock us
If, back when he was, we'd been current.

I guess it's just as well we weren't.

Why Dinosaurs Disappeared

With dreadful roars the dinosaurs
Bestrode their nests and tried
To hatch a heap of rotten eggs.
Their brainpans were not wide.

Had they been smarter, history
Might need to be re-inked.
If they'd just laid a fresher grade,
They wouldn't be eggs-stinked.

Ignatz
Pigfats,
    Round as a wheel,
Cried
To a fried
    Electric eel,
"You look
Like you need
    A good home-cooked meal!
How come
You dumb
    Eels grow so skinny?"

Said the eel, "He who swims
Soon slims,
    You ninny."

What We Might Be, What We Are

If you were a scoop of vanilla
And I were the cone where you sat,
If you were a slowly pitched baseball
And I were the swing of a bat,

If you were a shiny new fishhook
And I were a bucket of worms,
If we were a pin and a pincushion,
We might be on intimate terms.

If you were a plate of spaghetti
And I were your piping-hot sauce,
We'd not even need to write letters
To put our affection across.

But you're just a piece of red ribbon
In the beard of a Balinese goat
And I'm a New Jersey mosquito.
I guess we'll stay slightly remote.

How to Live in a Howdah

What's a howdah? A silk-curtained shack
Built to bounce on an elephant's back
Like a bottle abob on an ocean
Made of muscle in mammoth slow-motion.

How to climb to it? No way is straighter
Than by elephant-trunk elevator.
Drop a peanut in—up you will soar!
You get off at the very top floor.

Well then, how do you live in a howdah?
Sipping piping-hot bowls of clam chowdah.
While you're riding around—lucky you—
Holler down to your friends, *Howdah do!*

Brother's Snacks

My brother's always
Snitching snacks—
He once munched apples
Made of wax.

He's such a steady
Midnight snacker,
He doesn't miss
A soda cracker

And in our fridge
How old, cold chicken
Lights up his eyes!
How his steps quicken!

Is he a hog?
You want more proof?
He munches shingles
Off our roof.

He likes to lunch
On driveway tar
And slabs of spare
Tire from Dad's car.

From both his fists
Hot popcorn's dribbling—
He's what Mom calls
My nibbling sibling.

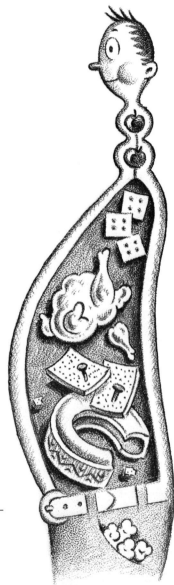

Little People's Express

A TALE FOR SAINT PATRICK'S DAY

In all Tipperary there wasn't one fairy
Who didn't feel jealous to watch jumbo jets
Arise out of Shannon like shot from a cannon,
So they caught a huge Junebug in gossamer nets.

Then with prodding and poking, to their seats in NON-
SMOKING
Between that bug's wings all those wee folk made
haste.
Snap your belts! yelled the pilot. *Lock the door to the
t'ilet!*—
And that flight down a runway of firefly-lights raced,

Lifted nose, did a wheelie, leaped to clouds white and
mealy
Where in daylily cups Steward Harebell served dew.
Said a bowlegged rainbow, *Will you look at that plane
go!*
'Twas the smoothest of flights till a wicked wind blew.

Little Biddy O'Banshee shrieked like some Comanche,
Och, we're set to splash down in a sea of green brine!
Meanwhile, back at the tower ('twas a cowslip in
flower),
They declared, *Some old owl must have swallowed Flight
Nine.*

But their plight wasn't terrible. Copilot Clarabelle
Urged them off the bug's back with the help of her
      boots
And like silk from a thistle, as slick as a whistle,
They unfurled their own wings and—bedad! all had
      'chutes.

Soon, the wind gently shifting, on down they went
      drifting
To a sweet field mist-glistening and buttercup-belled.
For emergency landing, sure, you'll have to be handing
First prize to the airline that's fairy-propelled.

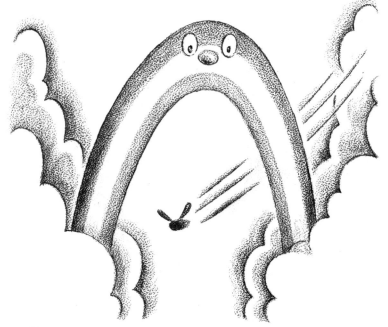

Backyard Volcano

Why oh why did an active volcano
   Have to poke up its snoot in our yard?
It goes *gloop* like a sink full of Drano
   And its showers of rocks sure hit hard.

From its crest you can gaze down on masses
   Of boulders that bubble and seethe,
Giving off gales of ghastly green gases
   That nobody's able to breathe.

"Balls of fire!" Uncle Jack yells, jackknifing
   Down into that smoldering cone,
"What a fine, steamy day to go diving!
   Last one in is an old molten stone!"

Now each night, with a cup of hot java,
   Mother props up her feet and feels snug
While she watches red rivers of lava
   Roll over our living-room rug.

Wildlife Refuge

After weeks of hard raining,
(In fact, hurricaning),
  When the world wore a waterlogged smell,
A sopping wet reindeer
Climbed out of his rain gear
  And made for a nice dry motel.

You shouldn't meet, according to all rules,
A short-eared owl, two common gallinules,
Some Barrow's golden eyes (chicks, cocks, and hens),
Eleven Lapland longspurs, seven wrens,
Nine snowy egrets, nineteen great white auks,
A rusty blackbird, sixty chicken hawks,
A red-rumped warbler and a whistling swan,
A flicker with his yellow slicker on,
Six evening grosbeaks and a northern shrike
Passing you on the Pennsylvania Pike—

But if you do, I bet that when you roll
Up to a booth a duck will take your toll.

Mom and Pop Ghastly Come Up for Air

The appearance of my parents
When they surface after weeks
Of hunting aardvarks underground
Elicits awful shrieks.

My parents burrow up and blink,
Their nails worn dull from digging.
Blue toadstools blossom from their ears—
It's dirty work, earth-pigging.

They haven't caught an aardvark yet
Although they've tried all year.
When I grow up I just might pick
A different career.

If you'd prevent a thunderburst
From washing all the liverwurst
Out of your sandwich (ham on rye),
Then munch your lunch indoors. Stay dry!
Who knows what *might* fall from the sky?

Why, one day seven years from now
As I sat sipping liquid cow
(That's milk) outside beneath the grass,
I got hit by a falling brass
Barometer and broke my brain.
That's what you call a heavy rain.

Poor Wicked Witch! Her broomstick stuck
Within a thick thorn thicket.
She tried and tried to thumb a ride
Upon some passing cricket.

By the highway side she could be spied
While midnight bells were striking,
With her green-eyed cat and her mean-eyed bat
And pointy hat, witch-hiking.

She cried, "By gum! my thumb is numb!
To bum rides makes me weary."
But at last a cricket skidded, stopped,
And hollered, "Hop on, dearie!"

So, seated on that cricket's back—
It felt like crinkly leather—
Witch held on tight and through the night
They thundered off together.

Since then, she's chopped her broomstick up
And never buys a ticket
On trains or planes. Down turnpike lanes
Witch whizzes on her cricket.

Said Gus Goop, "That spaghetti was great!
Only—where in the world is my plate?
    Something hard as a bullet
    Feels stuck in my gullet—
Could it be that canned tuna I ate?"

◆◆◆◆

In art class, I gasped. At the easel
Right next to me stood a huge weasel
    All wrapped up in his toils
    On a landscape in oils,
But his oil came in cans that said DIESEL.

◆◆◆◆

A luckless time-traveler from Lynn
Leaned too close for a look and fell in
    To a puddle of slime
    On the first day of time
And so, naturally, couldn't have been.

◆◆◆◆

Oh, how low can you go, Gosnold Goop?
Is there nothing to which you won't stoop?
    (Gosnold sees sinking ships off,
    Robs roach traps, and rips off
The S's from alphabet soup.)

◆◆◆◆

"Now just who," muses Uncle Bill Biddle,
"Drilled a dreadful big hole through my fiddle?
    When I play a folk air
    Air is all there is there
And my tune comes out minus its middle."

◆◆◆◆

On a day when the ocean was sharky
Archaeologist Arthur McLarky
    For a quick dip dived in,
    But along came a fin—
All they found was his shovel and car key.

◆◆◆◆

My Scottish great-granduncle Milt's
Favorite sport is to climb up on stilts
    And then stand on his head,
    Which arouses great dread
And the warning, "Don't do that in kilts!"

◆◆◆◆

An unusual man from Bound Brook
Used to hang up his coat on a hook,
    But what made him of note
    Is he kept on his coat,
That suspense-loving man of Bound Brook.

◆◆◆◆

Try seeing through shoes' points of view!
  Bend ear to hear your sneakers!
They've tongues to talk, and when they're new,
  Some shoes contain loud squeakers.

Suppose one day your shoes and you
  Should suddenly change places—
Then how would YOU like being *two*
  With feet inside your faces?

Through chewing-gum stuck to the street,
  Through snowdrifts when it's snowing,
Would you be happy hauling feet
  Wherever they were going?

Make friends with shoes. Nights when they lie,
  Worn from your day-long paces,
Be sure you feed them shoofly pie
  And licorice shoelaces.

Things on a Microscope Slide

Your sore-throat germ may say, "Heh heh,
I'm little! I can hide!"
Till a doctor grabs it by the tail
And slings it on a slide,

A kind of flat glass-bottomed ark
Where he collects, this Noah,
The eyes of flies, the knees of fleas,
The toes of protozoa.

I poke my parsnips through the place
    Where the wall has lost its plaster.
I used to poke them through my face,
    But now they go down faster.

The Dental History of Flossie Fly

Flossie, a stubborn little four-eyed
Fly, wouldn't ever take her fluoride
And, what is worse, refused to floss
Between her teeth (which grew green moss).
Her worried mom would urge her, "Brush!"
But she'd just answer, "Bosh!" and "Tush!"

One day while slurping sweet brown slop
From some abandoned lollipop,
She bit down hard and—bless my soul!—
A bit of food poked through a hole
In one back tooth and struck a nerve,
As those who do not brush deserve.

Poor Flossie gave the loudest buzz
That, since Creation, ever was
And fluttered off to Doctor Driller,
Who poked her jaw full of pain-killer
And patched that hole. Now Flossie rushes
After each meal and grabs six brushes—

One in each foot—and scrubs like crazy,
Up, down, around. No longer lazy,
She says, when offered peanut brittle,
"Thank you, I'll have a *very* little,"
And she, who once chewed all food fast,
Sees how long she can make it last.

In fact, no fly I know beneath
Both sun and moon has brighter teeth.

46

Walk with a bluebird in your heart,
Along life's highway ambling.
You'll always have an ample stock
Of songs, and eggs for scrambling.

Walk with a rainbow in each eye—
They'll light your way, I'm told,
And you'll find, hanging from each ear,
A big fat pot of gold.

Walk with a skunk beneath each arm—
They just might make you nervous,
But when you want to be alone
Those skunks will prove of service.

The Case of the Crumbled Cookies

Crime in the kitchen! Calling all cars!
A deed's been done—the cookie jar's

Smashed all to pieces! Crime of crimes!
Fresh cookies crumbled in their primes!

I'm summoned—me, Sam Supersleuth,
To snoop, sniff, and track down the truth.

I'll catch the culprit in a flash!
Hand me my wig and false mustache.

I take long, supercareful squints
And dust each crumb for fingerprints.

I think hard, seeing what makes sense,
And slowly eat the evidence.

Ah! Chocolate chips, it's plain to see,
Were what that crook liked best. Like me.

And—hmmm-m-m, his shoes were number nine,
Exactly the same size as mine!

The shelf was high, his will power low.
He dragged a chair up close—just so—

And, standing straight and tall, he stuck
His hand in—just like this—and struck!

To lift that lid took brutal force.
Good thing I've strength enough, of course.

My manhunt ends right at the shelf.
I snap the handcuffs on myself.

Be wary of the fairies.
They're fond of sneaky stunts.
They like to kidnap kids and leave
In place of them strange runts.

If suddenly your baby
Looks owl-eyed, weird, and wild,
And shakes a wasp's-nest rattle, you've
A changeling for a child.

OK, you foxy fairies,
If you're in hearing range—
Come take my squawky sister.
She sure could use a change.

No Grosser Grocer

You'll never know a grosser grocer
Than nasty Gnashly Ghastly, no sir!

By cabbages he's long been dreaded.
He chops their heads off, sells 'em shredded.

His margarine is seaweed-green.
Legs poke out of his eggs. Bad scene!

His pecan candies squirm and wriggle.
On jars of pickles, loose lids jiggle.

His coffeecakes look twelve years old.
Nothing he sells has yet been sold

Except to tribes of mangy trolls—
They like his mildewed jellyrolls!

But if *you* meet this real gross grocer,
Go home and hug your stuffed bear closer.

A scallion has a scad of skins
And like a birthday candle
It's waxy white. To take a bite
You hold it by its handle.

It grows in ground. You grab its top
And up comes, moist and muddy,
A scallion. When you've munched it, stop,
Don't blow on anybody.

A Tale of Two Cities

Oh, here's to the city of Frankfurt,
The place that frankfurters call mother,
Where one half of American cooking began.

Here's to Hamburg, the home of the other.

Sheldon the selfish shellfish
Stayed clamped shut in his shell
Till one day ailing Elmer Eel
Came by and rang his bell.

"Help, help!" the ill eel moaned, and keeled
Right over on Shel's stoop.
"Oh, please, you well fish, take me in
And make me chicken soup."

"What?" yelled the shellfish. "Chicken soup?
You ill eels have your nerve!
Why, hot boiled hen is lots more than
The likes of you deserve!"

A long, thin squeal, and Elmer Eel
Passed out without a word
And on the stoop seemed such a droop
That Sheldon's shut heart stirred.

"He shall be fed!" the shellfish said,
And tucking that limp eel
Into the longest oyster bed,
Shel rustled up a meal

And ladled hot hen soup till El
No longer looked a mess.
So let us, you and I, like Shel,
Get rid of shellfishness.

I've got the measles. Want 'em too?
I can give them to you eas'ly,
But though we share and share alike
Your share will still be measly.

Down the mountainside Bill Bolling
Set a little snowball rolling,

Rolling at so great a rate
That it quickly gathered weight,

Picking up head over heels
Skiers, bears, and snowmobiles,

Knocking pine trees down like jacks,
Sweeping freight trains from their tracks—

How it grew! It left, on landing,
A few sticks in the city standing.

"Guess that goes to show you, folks,"
Said Bill. "From little acorns, oaks."

But people roared, and started rolling
A whole new snowball round Bill Bolling.

Sister Has a Blister

Sister has a blister.
She looks like something hot
Came up to her and kissed her.
Did she sip from a pot

Of blazing cocoa? No sir,
That blister simply rose.
I sort of love my sister,
But oh! how that thing shows.

A porcupine
Is on the line—
He wants work. He keeps wheedling
How he's a whiz at scaring skunks.
He says, Do you need needling?

He says he'll come help pry your snakes
Loose from their last year's skins.
He'll pen you letters with his quills,
Slit open old unanswered bills,
And even cushion pins.

It seems the jobs he wants to do
Are sort of odd and funny,
But let's say, Fine!—
A porcupine
Deserves to make pin money.

Margaret K. McElderry Books
Macmillan Publishing Company
866 Third Avenue
New York, NY 10022
Collier Macmillan Canada, Inc.

Designed by Barbara A. Fitzsimmons
Printed in the United States of America
First Edition
10 9 8 7 6 5 4 3 2 1

Library of Congress Cataloging-in-Publication Data
Kennedy, X. J.
    Ghastlies, goops & pincushions: nonsense verse/X. J. Kennedy.—
1st ed.
        p.   cm.
    Summary: A collection of nonsense poems describing a variety of unlikely
characters and situations.
    1. Nonsense verses, American.   2. Children's poetry, American.
[1. Nonsense verses.   2. American poetry.]   I. Title.   II. Title:
Ghastlies, goops, & pincushions.
PS3521.E563G4   1989   811'.54—dc19   88–28663   CIP   AC
ISBN 0–689–50477–2